THE SYSTEM OF
SELF C.A.R.E.

4 Life Practices to
Improve Mental Health and Performance

DARRYLL STINSON

The System of Self-C.A.R.E.

Copyright © 2025

ISBN: 979-8-9915865-0-4

Printed in the United States of America

Thank you for your cooperation

CONTENTS

DISCLAIMER

This book is all about self-care and mental health, but I'm not a doctor, therapist, or mental health professional. I have learned the insights contained in this book from the practices I've used to battle depression and rebuild my life from a suicidal state of being to become the husband, father, and global leader I am today. While I truly believe these practices can transform your mental health and support your career success, my advice should not serve as a substitute for professional medical advice, diagnosis, or treatment.

Mental health and mental illness are complex, and everyone has their own journey. While the strategies in this book have helped me and others, they might not be right for everyone. If you're dealing with mental illness or having thoughts of suicide, please reach out to a qualified mental health professional immediately.

Remember, seeking help is a sign of strength, not weakness. If you're in crisis or having thoughts of self-harm, don't fight that battle alone. Reach out to a crisis hotline or a trusted friend, or head to your nearest emergency room or mental health care facility. Your life matters, and there are people ready to help as you find the courage to speak up and ask for the support you need and deserve.

This book is meant to complement professional care, not replace it. Think of it as a tool in your mental health toolkit, not the whole toolbox. Use it alongside professional guidance for the best results.

WHAT'S NOT IN THIS BOOK

Mental health is such a complex and often controversial topic. There are literally thousands of remedies, medications, practices, and other resources out there to help you improve your mental health and quality of life. I chose to only include solutions, or what I prefer to call practices, that I have used to work through my own mental health challenges. Some of these, such as medication, have intentionally been omitted from this book since that conversation is appropriate to have with a mental health professional. I wanted this book to be short and applicable so that people who are in crisis do not have to read a dictionary just to work through their mental health challenges. I also wanted to create something for the high achievers to be able to find an edge up by testing out some of these practices. Therefore, the topics listed below have not been included in this book.

MEDICATION, SELF-MEDICATION, AND PSYCHEDELICS

It's crucial to understand that seeking professional help and using prescribed medication for mental health issues is completely normal and often necessary. I learned in my journey that I could release the shame I had related to taking medication or experimenting with other medicines. It was truly no different than taking vitamin D to supplement my lack of sunlight or vitamin D-rich foods. The medications were attempting to supply something my body was lacking—and there is no shame in that. Be sure to consult a medical professional or multiple when exploring using medication, self-medication, psychedelics or anything like this. Remember, what works for one person may not work for another, and that's okay.

SUPPORTING A LOVED ONE WITH MENTAL ILLNESS

If you're married to or in a relationship with someone who has depression or another mental illness, know that you're not alone. Supporting a loved one through their mental illness can be challenging, but it's also an opportunity for growth and deeper connection. Communication, patience, and self-care are key. My wife, Brittany, and I have recorded several videos providing insights and encouragement to those who are in the trenches with loved ones battling mental illness. You can access these videos in our free resources bundle available throughout this book. Remember to prioritize your own mental health while supporting your loved one. Sometimes, if we are not careful, we'll neglect our own needs out of love for someone else, and over time, that doesn't work very well as we tend to run out of steam or feel depleted.

Grab the resources, but focus on yourself throughout engaging with this material, and you'll be in a much more powerful position to help those around you.

BONUS RESOURCES

Throughout this book, you'll find QR codes linking to additional content and helpful resources. Explore these materials for deeper insights and practical tools to support your personal and professional growth.

Enjoy!

Chapter One

NOT YOUR TYPICAL "SELF-CARE" RANT

I never imagined my life would take the turns it did.

Growing up, I struggled to fit in, and sports were my sanctuary—the one place I truly felt I belonged. My classmates constantly teased me for being a "black kid who talked and acted white," and even cruelly rated me as unattractive. But on the field, none of that mattered. My athletic ability earned me the respect and admiration I'd been craving.

By high school, I had become a top-tier athlete, excelling in football, basketball, and track. I poured everything I had into my athletic career, determined to become the best in the world. I truly believed I would be the next greatest athlete of all time, like Michael Jordan was and is still considered to be. My dedication paid off—I became a U.S. Top 100 athlete in both football and basketball, earning a full-ride scholarship to Central Michigan University's esteemed football program.

I'll never forget when my coach sat Antonio Brown and me down during our freshman year. "Fellas," he said, "it's not a matter of if you're going to the NFL, it's only a matter of when." He was hinting at the possibility of us leaving college early for the NFL draft. I couldn't believe it. I was a couple years away from having everything I always wanted.

But fate had other plans. Before the end of my freshman season, I severely injured my back. This injury marked the beginning of the darkest, most challenging period of my life. After spinal surgery, I declined my coaches' offer to focus on my education while still honoring my four-year scholarship because sports weren't just something I did. They were who I was.

So, despite the dangers of playing Division 1 football after my back surgery, I signed a liability waiver and returned to the field as a rotating starter just one season later. The problem was that I never fully healed. I masked my ongoing pain with opioids and marijuana.

The next two seasons were a blur. I started selling drugs, mainly weed and Adderall, statewide to cover my medical expenses. My daily routine became a cycle of painkillers, weed, workouts, drug sales, classes, and more drug sales. Weekends were for restocking supplies and wild partying.

I never spoke up about my pain, fearing I'd appear weak or lose my spot on the team. The physical agony was crushing, but not as devastating as my dreams of becoming a professional athlete slipping away. Without sports, I didn't know who I was. I believed I could be successful at another career, but I doubted that I would be as fulfilled as I was by athletic competitions. I was trying everything to keep my career alive—epidural shots, nerve killings, stem treatment, acupuncture, physical therapy, and more.

As my addiction worsened and my sense of self crumbled, I sank into a deep depression. Having once felt invincible on the field, I now found myself wanting to end my life, unable to see a way forward. I feared that I would find out that people only loved me for my athletic ability and status rather than for who I was as a person.

Ultimately, I would soon find that to be true.

During my junior season, I took so many opioids that they thinned my blood and caused my nose to bleed every time I made hard contact on the field, which was almost every play. Every time, I would shove some tissue or cotton balls in my nose and lie to my coaches telling them it was bad allergies. Eventually, with the development of what appeared to be a permanent hunch in my back, they caught on to my lies and kicked me off the team before the end of my junior season.

I also soon discovered that my girlfriend of four and a half years, whom I had thought I was going to marry, had gotten engaged to another man before she and I officially broke up.

My heart felt broken beyond repair. Losing sports and the woman I had hoped to marry brought **emotional challenge I had no skills to handle**. In addition, I wasn't receiving a tenth of the amount of attention I was used to from coaches, trainers, media, my teammates, the general school population, or the broader community—which made me feel like I didn't matter even more.

Sick of the pain, angry at myself for losing sight of my identity, and furious at the world around me, I sought relief and vengeance through self-harm. Eventually, I ended up in a psychiatric care facility in Detroit, MI after my last suicide attempt in a vehicle.

I outline this story and the surrounding circumstances in more detail in my book, *Who Am I After Sports?* which has helped so many athletes, leaders, veterans, etc., navigate through an identity shift or season of transition.

Thankfully, this psychiatric care facility would change my life forever.

Two major things happened while I was there:

1. I found faith and started to believe there was a bigger purpose for my life.
2. I was introduced to self-care and mental health practices. For the first time, I saw a counselor, a therapist, and a nutritionist. I did my first mindfulness exercise. I read my first personal development book.

THE POWER OF FAITH

Finding faith was so powerful because I realized how much of my struggle with depression went beyond losing my identity and dream career. It went much deeper. I was depressed and suicidal in large part because I was living my life without a deep sense of purpose.

I don't share this publicly often, but when I was nine years old, I had a vivid vision of the leader I was destined to be. Since I had this vision at a young age, I knew I was supposed to be a leader, creative person of great influence who made a major difference in the world. Even in my darkest moments—drunk, high, or engaged in destructive behavior—there was always this nagging feeling of misalignment that felt like a knot in my stomach.

Instead of listening to my body or the silent whisper I would hear in my head telling me I was meant for more, I ignored the guidance and suppressed it with drugs, women, and busyness. I acted as if I couldn't feel the emptiness that came from being misaligned with my true purpose.

Finding faith in that psychiatric unit was "thawing" from all those years of suppressing my purpose. I finally had the belief and courage to be who I was destined to be despite the adversity, exclusion, pressure, or responsibility that may come with that decision.

THE EVOLUTION OF SELF-CARE

Participating in self-care and mental health practices for the first time completely shifted my paradigm. I say this all the time on stages: "I had a system of success as an elite athlete, but I didn't have a system of self-care." I knew how to optimize my routine, set my mind for success, study film, be coachable, and outwork my competition, but I didn't know how to process my emotions, regulate my nervous system when triggered, or practice being in the present moment.

So, after participating in the mental health practices in the psychiatric unit, I made a commitment to build my life from the inside out with my purpose, values, and character as the driving forces, rather than trophies, money, and respect from others.

This way of life combined my system of athletic success with my evolving system of self-care, and the results were massive. Within a few years, our communications team at Central Michigan University won two national U.S. awards (#1 & #3) in higher education communications and marketing. I learned how to edit & produce magazines, commercials, newsletters, as well as marketing, communications, and public relations campaigns.

Later, I trained healthcare organizations to grow their businesses using world class marketing principles. I then published a best-selling book that's been sold on every continent and read by athletes from high school to multi-gold medal Olympians. I revitalized a church from getting ready to close its doors with seventeen older members to a growing diverse, multigenerational congregation. I delivered a TEDx talk that gained 2.1 million organic views in one and a half years.

Darryll's Journey to Self-C.A.R.E.

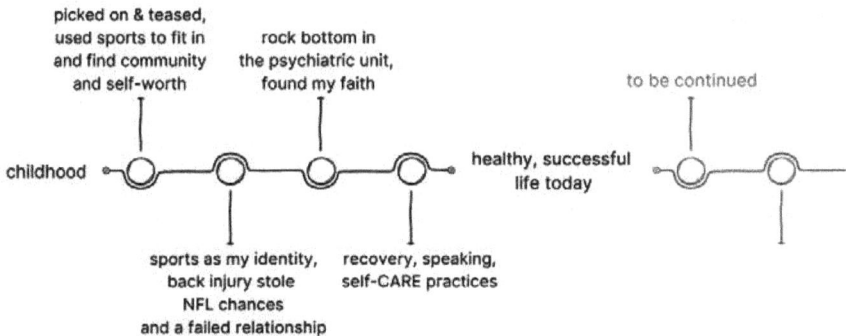

picked on & teased,
used sports to fit in
and find community   rock bottom in
and self-worth   the psychiatric unit,
found my faith   to be continued

childhood   healthy, successful
life today

sports as my identity,   recovery, speaking,
back injury stole   self-CARE practices
NFL chances
and a failed relationship

The best part is that I did all of this while learning how to be married, though I had never seen a healthy model, and raising four amazing children (three girls, one boy) and a dog named Magic. I built this success in my life without compromising my mental health by staying committed to self-care first. Not second, or in the margins of my life "when I have time." But first!

As I traveled the nation sharing my suicidal-to-success story and teaching others how to improve their mental health, I experienced many sleepless nights. I was on a mission to save everyone struggling with depression and suicide. To do so, I created dozens, and over time, hundreds of custom speeches related to my audiences' most pressing mental health challenges.

I was burning out from all the customization. I was desperate to find a way to combine the best of all that I was learning and teaching and put it into a simple, easy-to-remember, and easy-to-follow process for the sake of my own mental health and the audiences with whom I was sharing these insights.

I'll share with you how I came up with the Self-C.A.R.E. framework. First, I brain-dumped every mental health challenge that I had heard for nearly a decade from people all over the world and all varieties of industries and religious backgrounds. Literally, I wrote anything and everything that I could remember from when someone connected me to their loved one who was struggling with depression and suicidal ideation. I penned every frustration from leaders who were sick of mental health jargon that wasn't relevant or applicable for them. I recalled everything I could from audience members I spoke with who were desperate for hope and struggling to survive.

Next, I wrote down every solution that prevented me from attempting suicide again, and every mental health strategy I used to fuel greater levels of success and performance. I reviewed hundreds of testimonials, thousands of comments, and outlined every strategy or remark that people said was helpful to them.

From there, I organized the notes into categories such as medication advice, nutrition, breathing techniques, and so on.

Then I did the speaker thing and tried to compress all the information into an acronym, which would include either self-care or mental health. This way every time someone thinks of self-care or mental health, they can easily recall an acronym to help them overcome challenges they are having in that area.

I chose self care.

Conscious Awareness:

This is the practice of becoming more consciously aware of how your beliefs influence your behaviors so that you can more effectively and intentionally choose beliefs and behaviors that produce the results you want in life.

Activities:

This is the practice of moving your body to get in optimal energetic state so that you have more than enough internal strength, energy, and willingness to live and lead at your best.

Relationships:

This is the practice of nurturing and deepening your relationship with yourself so that you integrate that beingness into every relationship you have with people, and the world around you.

Expression:

The practice of giving voice to your talents, beliefs, and desires so that you have increasingly deep fulfillment and give your best to the world.

I'm not telling you because I think this is some type of genius strategy. Many people participate in brain dump clarity processes. I tell you this so you can understand that this process is not linear; you do not have to complete C before you work on A. It is a multidimensional process in which the components build on each other. The more you work on C, the more you grow in A, R, and E of the system and acronym.

Also, it's important to know how this acronym was created because some of the exercises within each C.A.R.E. practice do not match perfectly with the definition of that main practice or letter of the acronym. For example, the R in the acronym stands for relationships. I discuss the practice of deepening and nurturing our relationship with self, others, food, and money.

Some people have asked me, **"Why did you put food... with relationships?"**

I usually tell them it's because reflecting on our relationship to food has proven to be more conducive to people actually improving their food choices than talking about health benefits, facts, or dangers of certain foods.

The real reason is that how I improved my nutrition was more closely related to relationships than any other letter of the acronym.

I tell you all this so you can keep the backstory of how this method was created in your mind as you progress through this book. Remember, much like reading a manual about how to dribble a basketball, you won't develop your own skills until you start dribbling. Similarly, just reading this book won't likely make you start feeling better or see any change in your life or career—you have to implement the practices. Keep an open mind and a willing heart.

I'm excited to meet the next version of you!

Chapter Two

CONSCIOUS AWARENESS

Con·scious A·ware·ness
/ˈkänSHəs/ /əˈwernəs/

The practice of becoming more consciously aware of how your subconscious beliefs influence your behaviors—and intentionally choosing beliefs and behaviors that align with the life you desire.

Conscious awareness is the foundation of the Self-C.A.R.E. system. It's about waking up to your life and understanding how you operate. It's about deepening your understanding of why you make certain choices and how your past experiences shape your present beliefs and circumstances. Turn on the lights in the dark room of your mind and, suddenly, you can see more clearly what was right in front of you, but previously hidden.

Conscious Awareness:

Seats of consciousness

Brain scanning reveals that three areas of the brain play a pivotal role

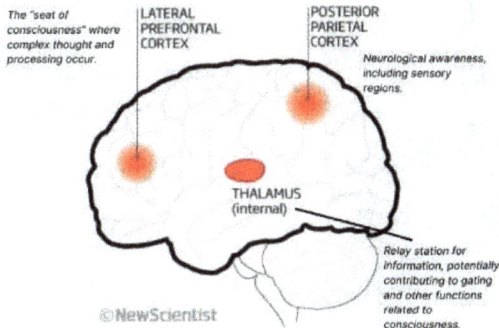

The "seat of consciousness" where complex thought and processing occur.

LATERAL PREFRONTAL CORTEX

POSTERIOR PARIETAL CORTEX

Neurological awareness, including sensory regions.

THALAMUS (internal)

Relay station for information, potentially contributing to gating and other functions related to consciousness.

©NewScientist

(Bor, 2013).

To share an example: For years, I felt anxious and uncomfortable when I was around people I perceived to be wealthy. Every time I was around someone with more money than me, I'd get this sick feeling in my stomach. My heart would start racing. My posture would shrink, and my typically booming voice would sink to a mumble. I'd even sometimes use self-deprecating language to deflect compliments and express how sad my life was. It was as if all my hard work, accomplishments, and my legitimate rise as a thought leader disappeared instantly as soon as someone with a higher net worth walked into the room.

I noticed a problematic pattern in my life. I would shrink around wealthy people or in environments where I couldn't afford the costs. This issue manifested in various situations—fundraising events, business meetings, and even restaurants with my family. The problem was consuming too much of my attention and energy.

It wasn't until I dug deeper that I realized what was really going on: I had a subconscious belief that I didn't belong around wealthy people. Throughout elementary and middle school, like a lot of young families, my parents couldn't afford to buy me all the clothes I needed to keep up with my growth. I was outgrowing every shirt, pant, and pair of shoes, which became expensive. They often bought my clothes that were two or three sizes too big so I wouldn't outgrow them so quickly.

My elementary school photo.
Notice the shirt is 2-3 sizes too big.

I would often feel embarrassed or out of place when kids in my school would sport new brand-name outfits the first week of school. Though I was sincerely grateful to have new clothes, they weren't the brands that everyone else seemed to be able to have. Anyone who had a similar experience growing up knows how much this affects a young kid trying to find themselves, handle peer pressure, and climb the social status ladder of public school.

Also, the wealthier kids in school could always afford the yearbooks, school portraits, paid field trips, and extracurricular activities. On the other hand, I would get in trouble for even asking about purchasing those things or attending those events.

I could name scenario after scenario where I felt this way, but, hopefully, you can see how this led me to believe that people who had more money than me were somehow more deserving or better than I was. I believed wealth was for people like them, not for people like me.

This belief was sabotaging my influence and ability to help others because I was blocking all the relationships, conversations, and events that made me feel this way.

Becoming aware of this pattern was the first step in changing it. Now, when I feel that old insecurity creeping in, I can take a deep breath to regulate my body's nervous system, stand tall, broaden my shoulders, and remind myself that I belong so that I can move forward with confidence.

And that's the person who starts to lead and build my life, opening opportunities for stages, collaborations, and community building projects.

HOW CONSCIOUS AWARENESS IMPROVES MENTAL HEALTH AND PERFORMANCE

Let's talk about why conscious awareness is such a game-changer for your mental health and overall performance. You know how sometimes you feel like you're on autopilot, just reacting to life instead of really living it? Conscious awareness is how you break free from the matrix of living life on repeat due to your subconscious programming and instead choose the life you want to create. It's how you live by design and not by default.

Red Pill:
New life you create

Blue Pill:
Life on repeat

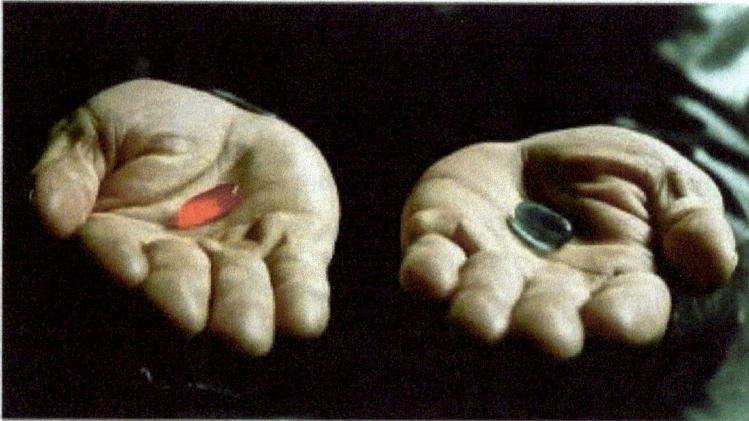

Photo: Courtesy of Warner Bros. (Taylor, 2011).

Would you drive a car blindfolded? I hope not. But that's kind of what it's like when you're not aware of your thoughts, emotions, and behaviors. When you take off that blindfold, when you choose that red pill of enlightenment—you become more consciously aware. Suddenly you can see the road ahead. You can steer. You can avoid obstacles. You're in control.

How does this affect one's mental health? Well, first off, it helps you catch those dark thoughts that can lead to depression before they spiral out of control. You know the ones I'm talking about. "I'm not good enough," "I'll never succeed," or "I'll never find love, acceptance, fulfillment, or _____ (you fill in the blank)."

When you're in a practice of conscious awareness, you can spot these thoughts and say, "Hold up. Where is this thought coming from?" And more importantly, "What is it that I want to think in this present moment?"

This is your internal guiding system for your thoughts and emotions:

Instead of overreacting or overworking when you're stressed, you start to recognize the early signs of your less healthy behaviors. Maybe your shoulders tense up when you need to have a crucial conversation with a team member, or perhaps your breathing gets shallow when you're on a tight deadline. When you notice these cues, you can breathe to regulate your body's nervous system, then make more empowering choices.

How many times have you made a "poor" choice and thought to yourself, "Why did I do that?" As we grow in the practice of conscious awareness, the speed of thought slows down for us and we make wiser choices vs. running on "auto-pilot" because we're busy or overwhelmed.

Conscious awareness is a game-changer for relationships, too.

Ever find yourself in the same argument with yourself or others over and over? That's a great place to examine what subconscious beliefs may be driving the behaviors that are creating this scenario in your life.

As an example, early in our marriage, my wife and I used to get into some pretty heated debates. When emotions would get high and the circumstances became tense, I often yelled, pounding my chest to assert that I was the man of the house and demanded that she not talk to me in a disrespectful tone of voice. You can imagine how ineffective this approach was in making my wife more loving and respectful towards me. Argument after argument, day after day, month after month, year after year, we kept having the same challenges. We'd disagree, emotions would flare up, voices were raised—mine the loudest, and I either shut it down or walked away.

Years of this repeated pattern finally shifted one day when I was in counseling. I was venting to my counselor about the latest disagreement with my wife, expressing my frustrations. My counselor looked at me and said, "Darryll, it doesn't sound like you're really angry."

"Oh yeah?" I retorted. "Because I sure do feel pissed."

"It sounds like the way your wife is talking to you is actually hurting your feelings more than it's pissing you off," my counselor replied.

I thought about it and realized that she was right. However, at that time, I was unwilling to own my feelings.

But as Dr. Michael Beckwith says, "sometimes pain has to push you until the vision pulls you."

The vision of what our relationship could be wasn't compelling enough to change my outbursts of anger—however, the pain of having the same argument repeatedly pushed me to try something different.
One day, in the heat of an argument, emotions were running high, my wife was raising her voice, and I was feeling all the frustration. Right before I had an outburst of anger, I stopped. I took a breath to calm down and said one of the most vulnerable statements I had ever uttered at that time: "You hurt my feelings." I tried to speak with my lips barely parting. It felt demoralizing, so non-manly, but it was true.

Explaining why my feelings were hurt was so challenging. I realized the reason I would get so angry and tense every time my wife would raise her voice at me during arguments stemmed from my childhood experiences. Growing up, whenever I got into trouble and tried to explain my behavior, I would get spanked or sent to my room. If I cried about any of these punishments, my parents would threaten, "You better stop crying, or I'll give you something to cry about." So, I learned to "bottle up" my emotions because it wasn't safe to express that I was hurt or felt misunderstood.

Years later, there I was, a grown married man lashing out at my wife, because, subconsciously, I was standing up for the little boy who never spoke up for himself when he was threatened and told to stop crying. I was also struggling to say that my feelings were hurt because it didn't seem to matter much growing up.

Becoming more aware of these types of patterns in my life and being willing to express my emotions vulnerably was a catalyst for my journey and my marriage. You can imagine how differently my wife responded to my hurt compared to my anger, and consequently how much better our relationship became.

Conscious awareness really is a superpower that gives you an edge in self-leadership, and relationships in general. You start to notice all these subtle ways you sabotage your own success, cause unnecessary stress, and suppress your emotions. Then you can intentionally choose the thoughts and behaviors that bring out your best.

This way of life leads to better mental health and improved performance, often in multiple areas of your life.

Conscious awareness isn't about being "woke" or making perfect choices all the time. It's about being present and moving with the flow of life — in a more empowering way.

Try it, once you start practicing this, you'll wonder how you ever lived any other way.

The importance of conscious awareness is highlighted in many bodies of research. I'm not just saying stuff because it sounds good; there are studies and research to back it all up. The Michigan Institute of Technology conducted a study with middle school students, which we all know could be one of the most stressful times in life. They found that when these students practiced being more aware, it actually calmed down the part of their brain that freaks out under stress (Trafton, 2019). It's like giving your brain a chill pill without the actual pill.

Other researchers found that regularly practicing this awareness "stuff" doesn't just make you less stressed - it can make you happier and more empathetic (Allen et al., 2021). It's like hitting the gym for your emotional well-being.

This skill is so valuable that the military has been integrating it into their training schedule for years. They found that being more aware helps people stay cool under pressure and perform better on the field of combat (Büssing et al., 2013). If our war heroes are taking this skill seriously while fighting real life-threatening battles, then imagine what it could do for you when you're dealing with work stress or that never-ending to-do list!

Being consciously aware isn't just some abstract spiritual concept. It's a powerful tool that can help you manage your emotions better, make smarter decisions, and just generally feel more on top of your game. It's like having a superpower, but instead of flying or invisibility, you get to be the boss of your own brain.

Remember, this is a practice, not a destination. It's something you cultivate over time, gaining more influence over your life with each insight. You move from being a passive participant to a more active creator of your life experience.

In the next chapter, we'll explore how to step into practices of moving our bodies to improve mental health and performance.

For now, let's pause and take a moment to experiment with what we've discussed.

Try It Out:

Here are some exercises to help you elevate your conscious awareness:

EMOTIONAL ACCOUNTING

- **SET A TIMER** for ten to fifteen minutes.
- **SIT UP STRAIGHT** Start by sitting up straight on an even surface and breathing deeply in through your nose and exhaling slowly through your mouth like you're blowing through a straw.
- **LIST YOUR EMOTIONS** Each day, list out your emotions for the first five minutes.
- **REFLECT** For the next five to ten minutes, ask yourself what's bothering you. What pain are you holding on to? What situations consistently trigger negative reactions?
- **RANK** these emotions by intensity, with zero meaning it doesn't bother you at all and a hundred meaning you have a very strong emotional spike when that emotion or memory comes up for you.
- **ORDER** the emotions from the ones with the highest score to the least. This process will let you become clearer on which emotions are bothering you and to what degree, rather than being emotionally entangled, confused, or conflicted.
- **BRAINSTORM** Then spend some time brainstorming ideas that can help you resolve whatever has come up in this process.
- **TAKE ACTION** Pick one to three actions and execute.

Daily Emotion Tracker Worksheet

Day: _____   Date: _____

Set a timer for ten to fifteen minutes when working through this worksheet.

LIST YOUR EMOTIONS (first five minutes)

1. _____
2. _____
3. _____
4. _____
5. _____

IDENTIFY TRIGGERS & RANK BY INTENSITY (next five to ten minutes)

What is bothering you? What situations consistently trigger negative reactions?

Intensity Score:
0 = doesn't bother you at all   100 = consumed by emotion

1. _____   Intensity Score: _____
2. _____   Intensity Score: _____
3. _____   Intensity Score: _____
4. _____   Intensity Score: _____
5. _____   Intensity Score: _____

ORDER EMOTIONS FROM HIGHEST TO LOWEST INTENSITY

1. _____

2. _____

3. _____

4. _____

5. _____

BRAINSTORM SOLUTIONS

Based on the emotions and triggers identified above, list potential solutions or coping strategies.

1. _____

2. _____

3. _____

4. _____

5. _____

ACTION PLAN

Choose one to three actions from your brainstorming session to implement.

1. _____

2. _____

3. _____

Reflection:

After completing the worksheet, what have you learned about your emotions and triggers? How do you plan to use this information to improve your emotional well-being?

_____

_____

PERSONAL CHECK-IN

- **SPEND FIVE MINUTES** each morning doing a personal check-in.
- **BREATHE** slowly through your nose for four to six seconds. Then slowly out your mouth like you're blowing through a straw for six to eight seconds.
- **MENTALLY SCAN** your body. Start at the crown of your head and work your way down to your feet. Notice any areas of tension or discomfort.
- **FOCUS ON THE TENSION** Wherever the most tension is, place your hand or draw your attention to that area of your body.
- **ASK YOURSELF** Breathe and ask yourself, what feelings are there? What emotions might be causing that tension in your body? When is the first time you remember feeling this tension in the body?
- **SPEAK OUT LOUD OR JOURNAL** about whatever comes up for you.

Daily Personal Check-In Worksheet

Day: _____   Time Started: _____

This is a five to ten minute exercise. Set a timer if needed, but don't worry about filling in every box. The goal is awareness, not perfection.

BREATHING EXERCISES

- Breathe slowly through your nose for four to six seconds.
- Exhale slowly through your mouth (as if blowing through a straw) for six to eight seconds.
- Repeat this cycle for one to two minutes.

BODY SCAN (two to three minutes)

Starting from the crown of your head, slowly scan down to your feet. Note any areas of tension or discomfort.

Body Part	Pain Scale 1-10	Notes
Head		
Neck		
Shoulders		
Arms		
Chest		
Back		
Abdomen		
Hips		
Legs		
Feet		

Area with the most tension: _____

EMOTIONAL CHECK-IN (two to three minutes)

Focus on the areas of most tension. Place your hand there or draw your attention to it.

As you breathe, reflect on these questions:

1. What feelings are present in this area?

    _____

    _____

    _____

2. What emotions might be causing this tension?

    _____

    _____

    _____

3. When was the first time you remember feeling this tension in your body?

    _____

    _____

    _____

Reflection:
Use the space below to journal about whatever has come up for you.

_____

_____

_____

_____

_____

_____

_____

_____

_____

Time Ended: _____

How do you feel after this check-in?

Use one word to describe your current state: _____

This practice helps you enhance your sensitivity to your body's signals and build a habit of expressing emotions that you tend to suppress. This emotional clarity leads to clearer awareness. It's like cleaning dirty glasses. You can only access the full vision by cleaning the lenses.

MEDITATION PRACTICE (five minutes initially, increasing over time)

- **SET A TIMER** for five minutes.
- **SIT UP STRAIGHT** Find a place where you can sit up straight in a distraction-free environment. Sit with your feet firmly planted on the ground, eyes closed, and arms and legs uncrossed.
- **BREATHE** slowly through your nose for four to six seconds. Then slowly out your mouth like you're blowing through a straw for six to eight seconds.
- **FOCUS** your attention only on the breath as you inhale and exhale. If any thoughts cross your mind, do your best to bring your focus back to your breath.
- **JOURNAL** When your five minutes are complete, journal about what the experience was like for you. How was your focus during the meditation? What thoughts or distractions did you notice?
- **ASK YOURSELF** What feelings came up for you? How do you feel after meditation compared to before?
- **SLOWLY INCREASE THE TIME** Start with five minutes each day for seven days. The following week, increase your time to ten minutes. The week after that, fifteen minutes. Keep following this increase until you reach sixty minutes, or as close as you can. Do not increase your time if you haven't been consistent every day or feel that you haven't consistently remained present during your mediation.

Meditation Worksheet

Weekly Meditation Tracker

Day	Duration (in minutes)	Completed	Notes
Sunday			
Monday			
Tuesday			
Wednesday			
Thursday			
Friday			
Saturday			

Progress Notes

Week 1 (five minutes daily): _____

Week 2 (ten minutes daily):_____

Week 3 (fifteen minutes daily): _____

Next Goal: _____ minutes daily

Remember:
- Sit with feet firmly planted, eyes closed, limbs uncrossed.
- Breathe slowly: four to six seconds in through nose, six to eight seconds out through mouth.
- Focus only on your breath. Gently redirect focus back to the sensation and movement of your breath when thoughts arise.

- Increase duration only if you've been consistent and present in your practice.

More Advanced Practices:

THIRTY-DAY SUBCONSCIOUS BEHAVIOR PATTERN TRACKING EXERCISE

The goal of this exercise is to identify and understand your subconscious behavior patterns by tracking your emotional reactions and associated thoughts and behaviors over thirty days.

Daily Practice:
- **IDENTIFY** Emotional Reactions
- Each day, **NOTICE and WRITE** down any strong emotional reactions, both positive and negative.
- **ANALYZE** Recurring Patterns
- For recurring patterns, **DOCUMENT**:
    - The initial emotion
    - Connected thoughts, feelings, or behaviors that occurred before or after the emotion
    - The surrounding context
- **SIMPLIFY** the Pattern
- **CONDENSE** the pattern into a simple sentence: "When I feel X, I react by doing Y."
- If needed, create a more detailed statement to **CAPTURE NUANCES**.
- **REFLECT** on origins
- **ASK YOURSELF**: "When was the first time I remember feeling this way?"

This often leads back to formative experiences that shaped the pattern.

Example: <u>Original Emotion</u>: Anger while driving

<u>Surrounding Context</u>:
- Rushing to work, feeling pressed for time

34

- Resentful about early start time compared to boss's schedule
- Another driver cut me off, nearly causing an accident

Reaction:
- Startled and angered
- Sped up to catch the other driver
- Rolled down window and yelled at them

Simplified Pattern:
- "When I feel pressured, late, and mistreated, I outburst in anger."

Detailed Pattern:
- "When I feel pressured by unfair guidelines and encounter anyone who isn't mindful of that, I outburst in anger."

Key Takeaway:
By consistently tracking these patterns over thirty days, you'll gain insight into your subconscious behaviors and emotional triggers. This awareness is the first step towards understanding and potentially changing these patterns.

Thirty-Day Subconscious Behavior Pattern Tracking Worksheet

Instructions:
Use this worksheet daily for thirty days to track your emotional reactions and associated thoughts and behaviors. This exercise will help you identify and understand your subconscious behavior patterns.

DAILY ENTRY

Date: _____

1. **Identify Emotional Reactions**
   List any strong emotional reactions you experience today (both positive and negative)

   - _____
   - _____
   - _____

2. **Analyze Recurring Patterns**
   For each recurring pattern, document:

   a. Initial Emotion: _____

   b. Connected thoughts, feelings, or behaviors (before or after)
      _____
      _____
      _____

   c. Surrounding context: _____
      _____

_____

3. **Simplify the Pattern**
    Condense the pattern into one simple sentence: "When I feel

    _____, I react by doing _____."

    Detailed pattern statement (if needed):

    _____

    _____

4. **Reflect on Origins**
    When was the first time you remember feeling this way?

    _____

    _____

    _____

WEEKLY SUMMARY

Complete at the end of each week.

Most frequent emotions:

1. _____
2. _____
3. _____

Most common patterns:

1. _____

2. _____

3. _____

Insights or observations:

1. _____

2. _____

3. _____

MONTHLY REVIEW

Complete after thirty days.

1. What feelings are present in this area?

   _____

   _____

   _____

2. What emotions might be causing this tension?

   _____

   _____

   _____

3. When was the first time you remember feeling this tension in your body?

   _____

   _____

   _____

4. When was the first time you remember feeling this tension in your body?

_____

_____

_____

Remember: Awareness is the first step towards understanding and potentially changing these patterns. Be patient and kind to yourself throughout this process.

ROOT BELIEF IDENTIFICATION

- Set aside ten minutes to **IDENTIFY THE ROOT BELIEFS** driving the recurring patterns. If you've been in the work of pattern tracking, then simply add to the identified pattern: "When I feel _____, I react this way _____ because _____ (insert root reason why)."

- It may help to go back to the place where you felt the emotion strong in your body. **FEEL INTO** that area. Following the **SLOW BREATHING** pattern, ask yourself, "When was the first time I remember feeling this way?"

- <u>The example could read</u>: "When I feel pressured by unfair guidelines, and encounter anyone who isn't mindful of that, I outburst in anger because growing up my parents always made me late for school and I could never do anything about it. So now, I tend to have unhealthy outbursts of anger when people make me feel the same way my parents did when I was younger."

Root Belief Identification and Rewiring Worksheet

Set aside ten minutes to identify the root beliefs driving the recurring patterns. If you've been in the work of pattern tracking, then simply add to the identified pattern:

"When I feel _____ , I react this way_____ because _____ (insert root reason why)."

It may help to go back to the place where you felt the emotion strong in your body. Feel into that area. Following the slow breathing pattern, ask yourself, "When was the first time I remember feeling this way?"

The example could read: "When I feel pressured by unfair guidelines, and encounter anyone who isn't mindful of that, I outburst in anger because growing up my parents always made me late for school and I could never do anything about it. So now, I tend to have unhealthy outbursts of anger when people make me feel the same way my parents did when I was younger."

ROOT BELIEF IDENTIFICATION

Date: _____

Root Belief Identification (ten minutes)

Identified Pattern:

"When I feel _____ , I react this way_____."

Example: "When I feel angry, I react by yelling because that makes me feel like I'll be heard."
Reflect on the origin of this feeling:

_____

_____

_____

_____

_____

_____

_____

_____

ROOT BELIEF REWIRE

Set aside five minutes to rewire one or multiple root beliefs that are producing results you don't want. Keep in mind that not all root beliefs are negative or need rewiring. There is value in identifying your healthy root beliefs as well so you can more intentionally leverage that identity to move your life and career forward.

"When I feel _____, I will choose to react _____
_____."

Using the working example, the rewired belief could read: "When I feel pressured by unfair guidelines and encounter anyone who isn't mindful of that, I take a deep breath or find a safe space and yell out loud to express my frustration."

The goal is to choose a healthier response more consistently in similar situations. This way, the old root belief starts to be replaced by a new one from the consistency of making a conscious choice rather than being blindly influenced by subconscious patterns.
Original Root Belief:

_____

Rewired Belief:

"When I feel _____, I will choose to react _____
_____."

<u>Why this new reaction is healthier</u>:

_____

_____

_____

_____

Download your free resources here!

Chapter Three

ACTIVITIES

ac·tiv·i·ty
/akˈtivədē/

The practice of moving your body to get in optimal energetic state so that you have more than enough internal strength, energy, and willingness to live and lead at your best.

Now, before you start thinking I'm about to lecture you on hitting the gym every day, I'm not. Yes, I was a high-level athlete who worked out regularly, but you will not have to follow challenging workouts to benefit from moving your body in the way we will discuss in this chapter.

We will touch briefly on how exercise benefits our mental health, performance, and overall well-being, but the primary emphasis on this practice is on how moving your body affects your energetic state—and consequently the quality of life you desire (Holmes, 2022).
That's the goal and the practice to deepen overtime.

That's it. No fancy equipment required, no gym membership needed. We're talking about using your body as a tool to change how you feel and therefore change how you show up in life and experience the world around you.

Have you ever been in a funk, then decided to go for a walk and suddenly felt better? That was you shifting your energetic state with activity. Let me share how I became more conscious of how activity improved my mental health and performance.
HEADS UP! We're about to dive into some pretty heavy stuff.

I'm going to be real with you and share some of my experiences with depression and suicidal thoughts. If you're in a place where that kind of talk might be too much to handle right now, no worries at all. Feel free to **skip to the yellow highlighted words** and continue your reading from there.

In fall 2012, I had just overcome my last suicide attempt and had exited the psychiatric care facility that changed my life. Yet I still struggled with my mental health after I was released. I frequently lay awake at night, restless from heavy depression. A voice in my head kept telling me, "Nobody cares if you are alive. People only loved you because they thought you were going pro. Nobody loves, knows, or cares about who you really are."

The voice went on and on, and on, badgering me. Emotionally, I felt like I was suffocating under a weighted thousand-pound blanket.

To move through this heaviness, I'd get up, go outside and start walking or running, no matter what the weather was like outside.

In moments where I was extremely stressed and feeling emotionally suffocated, I'd take off sprinting up the street—praying, worshiping, yelling, and talking to myself, no matter what time of the night or day it was. I can only imagine how some people who saw me doing this may have felt seeing some guy running, screaming, singing and yelling outside on the sidewalks, streets, parks, and trails.

The movement of my body shifted the energetic state I was in from a stagnant, heavy state of depression to a moving state of freedom, grit, and pride.

That simple activity of running or walking until I worked up a sweat and felt my heart rate go up, shifted my state from feeling overwhelmed to feeling open and ready to face my challenges. Movement creates the feeling that only comes from getting a good sweat in.

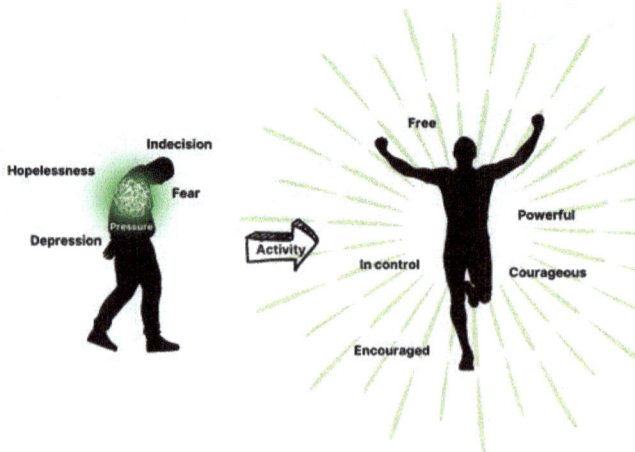

Indecision

Hopelessness

Fear

Free

Pressure

Powerful

Depression

Activity

In control

Courageous

Encouraged

The energy went from building tension within me to bringing freedom around me.

Activity isn't just about feeling better. It's about doing better as well.

Start Here:

When I transitioned from being an athlete to working a nine-to-five desk job, I felt claustrophobic and meaningless. I'd browse the internet instead of working more often than I should have, feeling unproductive and unfulfilled.

When you're dealing with emotional challenges, relational issues, or mental health struggles, you're less productive. You get distracted more often. You're not performing at your best. The average person works forty plus hours each week. Think about that. That's too much time in a person's life to feel like they're just going through the motions making sure they are paying their bills and saving/investing money for the occasional vacation and retirement.

So, I started experimenting with changing how I felt, since at the time I couldn't find a more fulfilling job. I'd play music at work, dance, and even get people in the office doing push-ups before meetings. Why? Because I wanted to change how we **felt** about what we were doing so that we could start experiencing the energy of our dreams in our work, which as a byproduct would result in us **being more effective**, innovative, and productive.

The practice of moving your body to get in optimal energetic state isn't just about feeling better, or "pumped up" for no reason. It's about **being better** so that you have enough internal strength, energy, and willingness to live and lead at your best.

HERE ARE A FEW ADDITIONAL EXAMPLES.

(Feeling better)   (Being better)

From Crisis   **to Calm**   **to Contributing**

We all have those moments when everything feels like it's crashing down around us. Whether your heart is racing because your bills are due and you're short on cash or your mind's spinning because you have a work issue you can't solve; in moments like those, step one is to move your body in a way that would help you to feel calm. Then you'll feel better in the midst of whatever is going on around you.

Now that you feel calm, step two is to move your body in a way that will make you feel like doing something to serve others. Depending on your personality and natural body impulses, these body movements can range from a slow brisk walk to full-on sprints, workouts, or extreme adventures. It all depends on the circumstances and makeup of the individual. Experiment and find what works best for you.

(Feeling better)   (Being better)

From Resistance   **to Readiness**   **to Ripping it**

Ever sit down to work and suddenly find yourself doing anything but the task at hand? That resistance is real, and it's powerful. When you're struggling to start a task, step one is to use movement to shift from "I don't want to" to "I'm ready and willing to." A quick dance break or a few stretches can help break through that mental and emotional resistance.

Once you're feeling better, step two is to do better by moving your body in a way that makes you feel like bringing your best to whatever task is before you. Just like an athlete would listen to music to get amped before a fierce competition to bring out their best performance, you can get yourself amped for the daily tasks at hand. And, no, writing emails can never compare to competing in the Olympics, but getting yourself moving and excited will definitely produce better emails. Take it from a guy who was listening to Eminem's "Lose Yourself" song just to write a newsletter and ended up winning a best newsletter in higher education award for our work.

You can move from resistance to readiness to ripping it in nearly every difficult circumstance or mundane task. But you have to allow yourself to. I know in seasons of intense pain or growth it can feel nearly impossible to make such a massive shift. But from my experience, that's what the pain in my life was there to invoke in me. Without the pain, I wouldn't have had enough internal resolve to try hard enough to push to higher levels of success. In my opinion, it's what Marianne Williamson is speaking to in her widely quoted book, *A Return to Love*, when she says, "Our deepest fear is not that we are inadequate. Our deepest fear is that we are powerful beyond measure." (Williamson, 1992)

Sometimes, subconsciously, I allow myself to get depressed and stressed about life because I am afraid of the influence, responsibility, and attention that comes when I let my light shine—or choose to bring my highest excellence to whatever task is before me.

Reflect on areas of your life where that behavior might be playing out...

Remember: you always have the power to change how you feel.

Once I started growing in the practice of "activities" aka moving my body to get in optimal energetic state, I became far more intentional, and my success and fulfillment started exceeding my expectations. I hope the same and more is true for you when you put this practice to the test!

Try It Out:
Practical Ways to Shift Your State

THE MOOD WALK

- **WALK BREAK** If you're feeling stuck on a problem or overwhelmed by your workload, take a ten- to fifteen-minute walk break.
- **MATCH YOUR WALKING PACE** to how you want to feel. Need to calm down? Slow down your breathing with longer inhales and exhales and walk at a slower pace. Want to feel energized? Pick up the pace to a jog or sprint.

THE MINI-DANCE PARTY

- **SET A TIMER** If you're feeling sluggish or resistant to an important task, stop and set a two- to three-minute timer.
- **PUT ON YOUR FAVORITE SONG**, turn up the volume as loud as you're able and dance like nobody's watching. Use headphones if you can't crank the volume up loud enough.
- **REENGAGE** After you start to feel more up for your task, reengage from a new state/energy level.

PERFORMANCE ENERGY OPTIMIZATION

- **PLAYLISTS** Create music playlists that will put you in the energetic state most conducive for your productivity or performance of your work tasks.
    - o As an example, upbeat music for tasks you don't enjoy doing, classical music for creativity, and calm instrumentals or Chillhop for focused work.
- **MOVE YOUR BODY** with the music if needed for the optimized state. For example, doing push-ups while listening to upbeat music prior to a typically boring meeting could transform the experience and elevate the results.
    - o Sixty-second minimum recommended.

FULFILLMENT ENHANCER

- **LIST** all your daily tasks for a typical week. It may help to go day by day.
- **RATE EACH TASK** on a scale of one to ten for how much joy/fulfillment it brings you.
- **BRAINSTORM** ways to increase how much joy/fulfillment you could have while doing each task. Could you add music? Movement? Make it a game? Or reframe your mindset?
- **ONE WEEK** Implement these changes for a minimum of one week.
- **REASSESS AND REPEAT** each week until the average score is where you want it to be. You don't need to go from a three to a ten in enjoyment. Even small increases can make a big difference when you consider how much time you spend on these tasks. The goal is to increase your average. A six may be a great target to start, since consistent tens are unrealistic and unachievable regardless of what any pseudo spiritual person tells you.

Fulfillment Enhancer Worksheet

Week Of: _____

Set aside ten minutes to identify the root beliefs driving the recurring patterns. If you've been in the work of pattern tracking, then simply add to the identified pattern:

STEP ONE: DAILY TASK LIST

List all your daily tasks for a typical week.

STEP TWO: JOY/FULFILLMENT RATING

Rate each task on a scale of one to ten for how much joy/fulfillment it brings you.

STEP THREE: JOY/FULFILLMENT IMPROVEMENT BRAINSTORMING

For tasks with lower joy ratings, brainstorm ways to increase enjoyment.

Consider:
- Adding music
- Incorporating movement
- Making it a game
- Reframing your mindset

STEP FOUR: IMPLEMENTATION

Implement these changes for one week.

STEP FIVE: REASSESSMENT

After one week of implementing changes, reassess your joy/fulfillment ratings.

.

Day	Tasks	Joy Rating	Ideas to Increase Joy	New Rating
Mon				
Tues				
Wed				
Thurs				
Fri				
Sat				
Sun				

Average joy/fulfillment rating: _____ / 10

Reflection:
What worked well? What didn't? What will you try next week?

_____

_____

_____

_____

_____

Next Steps:
- Repeat this process weekly.
- Aim for an average fulfillment rating of six or more to start.
- Remember that small increases make a big difference over time.
- 100% joy is unrealistic; focus on improvement, not perfection.

Chapter Four

RELATIONSHIPS

re·la·tion·ship
/ri-ley-shuhn-ship/

The practice of nurturing and deepening your relationship with yourself so that you integrate that beingness into every relationship you have with people, and the world around you.

RELATIONSHIP WITH YOURSELF

Your relationship with yourself is the foundation for everything else in your life. I learned this the hard way. After multiple attempts to end my life while battling depression, I realized I had buried my true self beneath layers of false identities I'd created to fit in. I changed everything about myself—the way I talked, looked, the music I listened to, how I dressed, even how I laughed. I did all this to gain acceptance from the "street" kids in my community.

And you know what? It worked. I got street cred and respect. Some of my peers came to know me as this "kingpin" figure. However, the more I ignored my own desires and continued this pattern of doing whatever I could to fit in, the further I got away from who I really was on the inside. By the time I came out of my "not wanting to live" phase, I was trying to find myself buried beneath all these layers of masks and fake identities.

DISCOVERING AND DEEPENING YOUR RELATIONSHIP WITH YOURSELF

I started taking myself on "me dates," going to movies, restaurants, and adventures alone. I was intentional about taking time to listen to my thoughts and emotions. At first, it was extremely uncomfortable to be alone with my thoughts. I was so used to constant noise and distractions—selling drugs, coaches checking on me, classes, parties, etc. Then later as I shed those toxic habits, I replaced them with work busyness, social media scrolling, eating unhealthy foods, etc.

Being alone with my thoughts for even two minutes felt too emotionally overwhelming. The moment I was quiet, my mind would start racing and my heart beating rapidly. All my insecurities and negative self-talk would start chattering faster and louder.

To create a sense of safety and manage the anxiety I experienced when I was by myself with no distractions, I set timers to push myself.

"Just see if you can make it five minutes meditating."

"Okay, Darryll. Try journaling for two minutes and if it's too much to deal with, you can stop. At least you can say you did it!"

I led myself to make incremental gains. In most cases, prolonged seated time with my thoughts and emotions was still too overwhelming emotionally and physically. So, whenever I would get stuck or triggered, I'd say, "Just take a walk and talk it out, Darryll. That's better than nothing."

During these walks, I'd talk in my head or out loud to myself. "How are you feeling, Darryll? What's on your heart and mind right now?"

This process was, and continues to be, a healing process for me. I began to hold space to listen to my voice and heart for the first time in more than ten years, rather than suppressing my thoughts and emotions to be accepted, loved, and respected by my peers. It felt tearfully, painfully good! I would get flooded with emotions and, in the spirit of expression, start yelling affirmations or prayers or running to move the energy rushing through my body. It was exactly what I needed at that moment to shift my energy.

This self-connection had a profound impact on my mental health. I became less dependent on others for validation, which improved my relationships. My performance in all areas of life improved because I was coming from a place of self-understanding and self-acceptance.

Building a deepening relationship with yourself is not much different than building a relationship with others. The same way you'd build a relationship with another person through shared experiences and conversations, "me dates" were my way of being intentional about building a relationship with myself. If you are not already in a deep practice of cultivating your relationship with you, then I invite you to test this out for thirty to ninety days to see what beauty and enrichment you might find.

THE "MAN IN THE MIRROR"

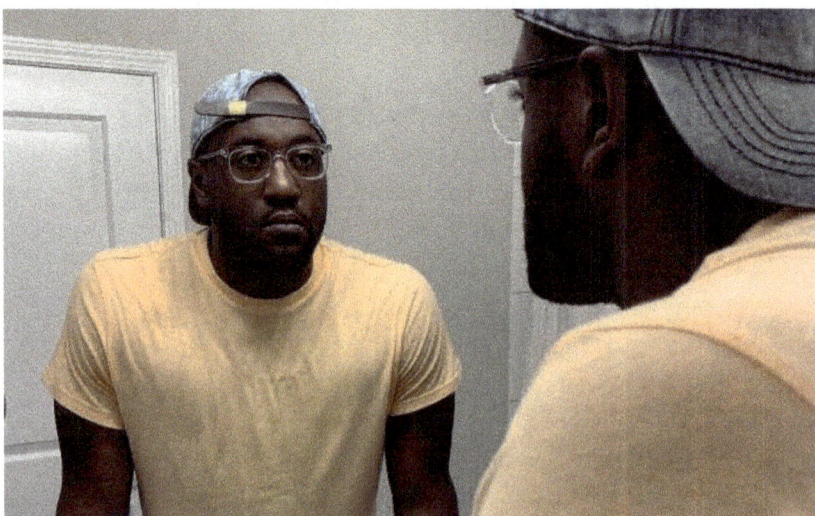

Mirror work was another powerful tool I found helpful in my journey to discover and deepen my relationship with myself.

It's a powerful practice that can help you form a better, more connected relationship with yourself. You stand in front of a mirror, look yourself in the eye, and speak positively to yourself. The key is to move beyond shallow compliments into speaking genuine, meaningful truths about who you are. It's a face-to-face connection with yourself, addressing your true value, potential, and who you are at your core. If you've ever felt lost, like you don't know who you are anymore, or have simply had trouble making a decision, this practice can help.

Mirror work gives you an opportunity to connect with yourself on the deepest of levels. We're often our own harshest critics. We tend to look in the mirror and see everything that's wrong with us. But this practice allows you to look beyond those imperfections, failures, and flaws to learn to love yourself for all of who you are.

I'll be honest, as poetic as that may sound, it was not easy for me to start out.

When I first started mirror work, I noticed how I hated looking at myself in the mirror. Every time I looked at myself, all I could see were my imperfections, failures, and bad decisions. I saw the large gap between my two front teeth and could still feel the sting from students' paper footballs hitting me in the face as they attempted a "field goal." I saw the darkness of my skin and recalled every moment when my teacher turned off the lights in class to watch Bill Nye and inevitably some student would yell, "Hey, where did Darryll go!? Oh, there he is! All we can see is his teeth and his eyes." At first, I couldn't even maintain eye contact with myself because of the shame I felt from those experiences and my own poor choices to sell drugs, cheat on women, and steal things.

For some reason, though, I kept feeling drawn to stare at my own reflection. There was a small part of me that, despite the shame I felt and triggers I experienced, could see and sense that beneath all this regret and embarrassment was my true self. I could see deep love in my eyes if I gazed long enough to see past the layers of guilt. I could see joy, confidence, and even my silly inner child as I gazed deeper and deeper into my reflection. Over time, the triggers weakened, and the antagonizing voices silenced enough that I could finally be with my own reflection. I was healing my relationship with myself, and I invite you to do the same. Whether you're filled with embarrassment, guilt, and shame, or you're wanting to take your relationship with yourself to new levels of confidence and connection, mirror work may serve as a powerful technique you can use to deepen your relationship with yourself.

YOU REALLY DO MATTER. IT'S NOT JUST CLICHÉ.

One of the main things that was causing me depression was this constant narrative in my head that there wasn't anything special about me.

Even though I had many people in my life tell me that I was amazing, called, and gifted, I didn't think I had any real, exceptional gifts outside of my athletic ability. I hid behind the persona of an athlete and a street thug so long that I had lost touch with myself and my innate skills and desires.

I labeled this thought pattern as one of the five lies of depression.

Lie #5: "There's nothing special about you."

You can access the rest of the Five Lies of Depression in the Free Resources chapter near the end of the book.

You can imagine how my belief that there wasn't anything special about me would negatively affect my mental health and performance.
To combat that lie, I went on a journey of self-discovery and assessment. I took every personal assessment I could find: Myers-Briggs, StrengthsFinder, Human Design, Enneagram, Spiritual Gifts, and countless purpose and self-discovery tests, guides, and experiences. This wasn't just about learning myself. At a deeper level, it was about finding a will to live, because in my mind (like many who battle depression), my life was pointless if I was just like everyone else. My thought was always, *if I really mattered and was so called and gifted like everyone says I am, then there should be something for me to do that only I, Darryll Stinson, could do!*

So, what was it!? I thought it was sports. I was extremely good at that! But that wasn't an option because of my back surgery, so what was it!?

MINDFUL PAUSE

This train of thought that "I feel like I don't matter because I don't have _____" is one of the most common narratives for people struggling with suicidal ideation.

If you know someone who might be dealing with these feelings, try to help guide them on a journey of self-discovery. Assist them in uncovering who they really are and identifying their unique talents, gifts, or purpose. This can be a powerful way to counter such negative thoughts and remind them of their inherent value.

So, there was a season when seeing the answers from one of these assessments gave me enough hope to keep living another day.

For example, when I was working in higher education as a community, I took the StrengthsFinder assessment and scored the highest for the strength of Harmony.

StrengthsFinders details how people with the Harmony theme are natural peacemakers who love finding common ground in any situation. They excel at bringing people together, solving problems practically, and calming tensions with their diplomatic skills. However, they might avoid conflicts too much, leading to unresolved issues or over-compromising. Sometimes, they even hold back their own opinions just to keep the peace.

I read the summary, strengths, and weaknesses and resonated with the majority of the descriptions, which helped me to exchange the thought of "there's nothing special about me" with "Oh, I have some strengths that are unique to me and could be useful for others."

The same thing happened with almost every assessment I took. Each result made me feel like I mattered and gave me enough hope to keep living another day or until I had the next depressive episode.

Did you catch that language? *Episode.*

Sometimes I tell myself that depression is just an episode. Yes, an episode. Like the ones you watch on television—which means it has a start and end time. That little reminder helps me not spiral deeper into the dumps and survive the depression like a storm that passes. This idea isn't meant to gaslight anyone or oversimplify a serious matter, so please seek out medical counsel or dismiss this description of depression if it doesn't resonate with you.

Depression and how your relationship with yourself affects your mental health and performance are definitely a much larger conversation that we can go deeper into with the provided resources. But for now, focus on "me dates," mirror work, and self-discovery assessments while not letting those episodes or challenging days get in the way of deepening your relationship with yourself.

RELATIONSHIP WITH OTHERS

As I was deepening my relationship with myself, I was able to approach my relationships with others in a healthier way. I realized I had been expecting too much from individual relationships, trying to get all my needs met by one person.

I had a mentor who was helping me develop and grow. He gave me my first leadership development books, and I started to think he knew everything about everything. I expected him to have answers for my finances, my marriage, my spiritual life, how to fix the VCR/DVD player—I mean everything. Whenever I felt lonely or had a question, he was the only person I'd reach out to aside from Google.

At the same time, I was pastoring people who were having the same unhealthy expectations of me. They also wanted me to be their everything: prayer partner, ideas person, spiritual guide, financial advisor, friend, and more. If I didn't show up to their baby shower, they would be offended. If I didn't want to perform a wedding ceremony or, God forbid, pray with them, then they would often take it personally. I realized this expectation for one person to be everything for someone isn't a healthy way to do relationships.

I learned to spread my expression and emotional weight across multiple relationships, understanding that different people serve different purposes in our lives. I started to see my pastor as my spiritual guide, my best friend as someone to have fun with, and so on. This shift in perspective dramatically improved my relationships. I was less needy, more appreciative, and able to nurture relationships in a more intentional way.

BEWARE OF FAMILIARITY: EVERY PERSON IS BRILLIANT IN SOME WAY

Another important habit that helped me cultivate quality relationships was to intentionally look for the brilliance in other people regardless of how familiar I became with their weaknesses or flaws.

It's easy to start to take for granted what you once were in awe of. Just like we can forget to express the appreciation we have for our beating hearts, we tend to get so familiar with those who are closest around us that we stop honoring their unique qualities. Maintaining that sense of appreciation and admiration is crucial for long-term, healthy relationships.

It can be challenging to learn how to honor and remain open to feedback from a colleague who is a mindset coach when I've seen them wimp out of a cold plunge or completely crumble on stage, but when I focus on their gifts instead of their flaws, I show up better in our relationship. Rather than have a less fulfilling relationship marked by indifference or stagnation, I experience a deeper love, openness, and connection that only flows where honor and receptivity are present.

Now that we've explored our relationship with ourselves and others, let's turn our attention to another crucial, yet often overlooked relationship—the one we have with food.

Yes, food.

HOW'S YOUR RELATIONSHIP WITH FOOD?

Your relationship with food can have a significant impact on your mental health and performance.

I heard a lot of people talk about intuitive eating and a more relational way of interacting with food, but it always seemed like they were being extreme. Then one day, while we were eating lunch at a personal development event, a friend of mine noticed I was eating very fast.

"Yoooo, slow down there, big boy. Your food isn't going anywhere," he said, smirking with a chuckle.

"What do you mean?" I asked.

"Usually when someone is eating that fast it's because they are trying to avoid something emotionally," he remarked gently, seeming to be trying not to trigger me.

"I'm not avoiding anything emotionally! We haven't eaten all day, and I'm hungry! What's the big deal?" I asked, feeling defensive.

"It's okay, my guy. I'm just here to help. If you're not trying to avoid anything, how about you try taking sixty seconds between each bite?" he said.

"*Easy.* I'll do ninety seconds! Two minutes! No biggie!" I said with arrogance.

I took a bite of food and waited for what felt like two minutes then checked my watch.

Only thirty seconds had gone by!

No way!

Time was moving too slowly! I held my composure so my friend wouldn't see me getting anxious. I tried to join other conversations at the table, but people were talking too much without pausing so I was "stuck" having to be with all my feelings. I started feeling left out. I started having flashbacks to the times growing up when I would eat lunch standing in the hallway by myself and then roam the halls so I wouldn't have to try to find a seat at a table, only to have someone make fun of me or tell me to go away.

Sixty seconds.

By the time that I got to ninety seconds, I was in a slight sweat from trying not to feel all the emotions that were coming up when I wasn't suppressing with food.

My friend just smiled at me. He already knew I was struggling.

This began an awakening for me of realizing how much I was using food to stuff down emotions rather than actually nourishing my body. I was eating fast, not even enjoying the taste of my food. I was trying to fill a void that had nothing to do with physical hunger. When we're overwhelmed emotionally or are in social settings that make us anxious, we often turn to food for comfort or distraction, or to numb our unwanted feelings. We eat mindlessly, barely aware of how what we're putting into our bodies is affecting the health we say we cherish.

People talk about "comfort foods" and use them to help soothe emotions. I've found them to actually be "discomfort foods" because of how they make us feel afterward or in the long-term. We've created positive associations with foods that are actually causing discomfort and disease in our bodies. Think about it how many times you have reached for a pint of ice cream when you're feeling down only to have the same emotions you were trying to avoid rushing back a few hours later or the next day?

Many of you have heard and used the term "hangry." Believe me, I have had my fair share of hangry moments. But if you're so attached to food that you can't behave nicely when you're hungry, I'm going to tell you from experience it's likely a sign that your relationship with food is off-balance. Consuming food in a healthier way means you're eating what your body needs to function optimally, not using food to fill every emotional discomfort. Our tendency to emotionally eat often stems from a lack of emotional regulation skills or difficulty in managing stress—again, pointing back to our relationship with ourselves and how we lead ourselves through discomfort.

But here's where it gets really interesting. Food also has a massive impact on your emotions and brain function, not to mention the obvious body functions. The gut-brain connection is real, folks. What you eat doesn't just affect your waistline; it affects your mood, your ability to focus, and more.

For example, foods high in sugar and processed carbs like white bread, pasta, baked goods, soda etc., can lead to rapid spikes and crashes in blood sugar, which can affect our mood and energy levels ("Carbohydrates and Blood Sugar," 2024). On the other hand, a diet rich in vegetables, fruits, whole grains, and lean proteins can provide steady energy and the nutrients your brain needs to function optimally.

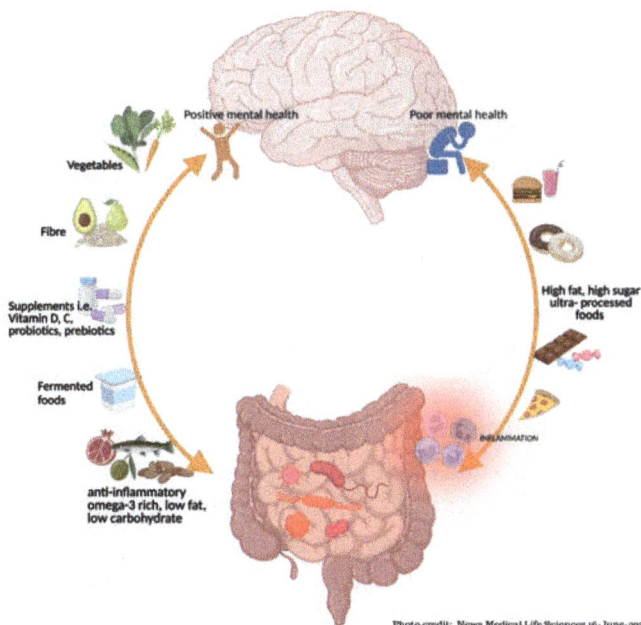

Photo credit: News Medical Life Sciences 16-June-2022

Changing my relationship with food to one of mindfulness and intentionality not only improved my physical health but also my mental clarity and emotional stability. It can dramatically shift your food choices and how you feel and perform.

So, let's change the narrative we've built around food and our dysfunctional relationship with what's on our plates.

Mindfully approaching eating has helped me tune in to my body's actual needs. I started to recognize true hunger versus emotional eating. I began to appreciate the taste and texture of food more, which naturally led me to choose more nourishing options.

Moreover, I noticed how my relationships with others affected my eating habits. When I was stressed about a conflict or feeling lonely, I was more likely to overeat or choose unhealthy foods. As I improved my relationships and learned better ways to handle stress, my eating habits improved as well.

Remember, your relationship with food reflects your relationship with yourself and others. It's all connected. By improving one area, you often see improvements in the others.

So, as you work on your self-relationship and your connection with others, pay attention to how your eating habits change. And vice versa—as you develop a healthier relationship with food, you might find it easier to connect with yourself and others.

LET'S TALK ABOUT MONEY

So much of our mental and emotional stress is connected to money. So many of our business and personal problems could be solved, or at least minimized, if we had more money. I can't tell you how many hours of counseling I spent worrying about money, or my lack of belief in myself to generate more of it. I wish I could track how often companies complain about money.

Here's what I know to be true: when I changed my relationship to money, money changed its relationship with me.

I first heard business expert Codie Sanchez say, "Money is a cruel mistress. If you don't pay attention to her, she'll leave you for someone who will."

I mentioned earlier in this book about some of my limiting beliefs around money. Those beliefs led to me having a very unhealthy relationship with money. I hated budgeting and making financial decisions. As an entrepreneur, I struggled to quote double- and triple-digit prices for my services. I felt uncomfortable around many millionaires and billionaires, even if they weren't full of themselves and were very approachable/relatable.

All that started to rapidly change when I realized one of the fastest ways to have more money is to change your relationship to it.

So, step 1 was to see what was causing friction in my relationship with money. I examined my beliefs, my parents' beliefs, and the beliefs of those who were closest to me, and started noticing a lot about peoples' relationship with money and how it influenced their net worth. It was obvious that people who had more money most often had a better relationship with money.

The next step after learning about my money beliefs was to improve my relationship with money by spending time with it daily.

Once I started tracking my spending daily and journaling about my feelings around money, I was able to make the necessary improvements to my budget and my mindset.

When you focus on your relationship with money, you start to clean up whatever mindset or unhealthy emotions are in the way of you having more of it. Try this approach to see what you might learn and experience.

Try It Out:

Here are some practices to help you grow in your practice of nurturing and deepening your relationship with yourself so that you integrate that beingness into every relationship you have with others and the world around you.

RELATIONSHIP WITH SELF

1. Self-Relationship Exercise: "Me Dates"
- **MAKE A LIST** of things you like to do.
- **SCHEDULE TIME ALONE** with yourself for a minimum of sixty minutes per week. I'd recommend over multiple days, though you can do that in one day.
- **CHECK IN** Use this time to check in with yourself, journal, or just be with your thoughts or have some fun if you're choosing to play a game by yourself.
- **JOURNAL** about what you learned and experienced.

2. Self-Relationship Exercise: Mirror Work
- **SET A TIMER** Set a thirty- to sixty-second timer.
- **LOOK AT YOUR FACE** close up in the mirror.
- **SPEAK GRATITUDE** As you relax, say one thing you're grateful for about yourself each time.
- Note: If you struggle with shame like I did, give yourself grace. Remember, it's a process that you're new to learning. Be patient with yourself. You will get better.

RELATIONSHIP WITH OTHERS

1. The Intentional Relationship Guide:
- **LIST** your top five closest relationships.
- **DESCRIBE** what you believe to be the primary purpose or reason that person is in your life.

- **LIST** Make a list of ideas about how you can improve the relationship to more accurately meet the depth of vision you see for your relationship with this person.

This will help you start to intentionally nurture your relationships vs. unconsciously expecting one person to fulfill all your needs or unconsciously slipping into stagnation. This helped me approach each relationship with intention and appreciation for what it uniquely offered.

The Intentional Relationship Guide Worksheet

Instructions:

Use this worksheet to map out your closest relationships, understand their purpose in your life, and brainstorm ways to improve them. This exercise will help you approach each relationship with intention and appreciation for what it uniquely offers.

1. **List Your Top Five Closest Relationships**
2. **Describe the Primary Purpose or Reason for the relationship**
   For each person listed above, describe what you believe to be the primary purpose or reason they are in your life.
3. **Brainstorm Ideas for Improvement**
   For each relationship, list ideas about how you can improve it to more accurately meet the depth of vision you see for your relationship with this person.

Relationship	Purpose	Improvement Ideas

Reflection

After completing this exercise, what have you learned/observed about your relationship or the time/energy in your life they consume?

_____

_____

_____

_____

_____

_____

_____

_____

_____

Remember: This exercise is designed to help you intentionally nurture your relationships rather than unconsciously expecting one person to fulfill all your needs or being unclear as to how to intentionally move your relationships forward.

A simple tip I learned was to ask myself, "What's the purpose or vision of this relationship?" before interacting with someone.

RELATIONSHIP WITH FOOD

1. Mindful Eating: Try the Sixty-Second Challenge

- **ONE MINUTE BITES** Take a full minute between each bite during your next several meals.
- **NOTICE** what thoughts and emotions come up at this time.
- **JOURNAL** about what came up for you during this experience. Were you as hungry as you thought you were? Were there any emotions you felt that you were using unhealthy food to suppress, comfort, soothe, or avoid?

2. Intuitive Eating

- **ASK YOURSELF** Before eating, ask yourself, "How do I want to feel when I'm done eating?" Then choose foods that align with that desired feeling.
- **WATER** Or, when you're feeling hungry, drink some water, take a few deep breaths and ask, "What does my body want right now?" Try waiting until you feel an internal "nudge" from your body or until a tasty, healthy food comes to mind.

RELATIONSHIP WITH MONEY

1. Money Journaling

- **WRITE DOWN** your thoughts, feelings, and experiences with money.
- **REFLECT** on questions like:
  - "How did my parents relate to money? What were some of those beliefs? What do I notice about my money beliefs when I observe theirs?"
  - "When I observe my body when I talk about money or my ability to generate more of it, what do I notice?"
  - "How would I describe my relationship with money in one sentence?"

2. Money tracking challenge

- **RECORD** For one month, record every single purchase you make each day – no matter how small.
- **JOURNAL** At the end of each day, journal about your expenses, why you made them, and more importantly what feelings were present while doing so. Every transaction doesn't need a journal entry, but for best results, think through every transaction to observe what you notice.
- **REFLECT** At the end of the thirty days, reflect on your experience and make notes on how you can improve your relationship with money. You don't have to wait till the thirty-day mark to start making improvements, but it's OK if you do.

Chapter Five

EXPRESSION

ex·pres·sion
/ikˈspreSHən,ekˈspreSHən/

The practice of giving voice to your talents, beliefs, and desires so that you have increasingly deep fulfillment and give your best to the world.

Let me tell you about the first time I realized how important the process of expression was for me. I went through a season where I was speaking to groups of people recovering from addiction multiple times every week, helping them to change their lives. At each engagement, though, I could feel that I wasn't connecting with some people in the audience I knew I could help.

Desperate to help these audience members who were fighting for their lives, I studied communication, hired coaches, read books, and did whatever else I could to learn about public speaking to fix the problem, but nothing was working. I was certainly becoming a better communicator, but I was still not resonating with a good portion of the audience. I couldn't figure out why, and it was tearing me apart.

Then one day it hit me: The reason I wasn't connecting with this audience was not because I wasn't a great speaker with wisdom to offer. It was because I wasn't being vulnerable enough to let the audience know I could relate to them. And most people recovering from addiction that I know won't listen to your advice if they don't feel like you can relate to them.

You see, I was trying to be this perfect, polished speaker—pausing at the right moments and making everything sound "tweetable." I was afraid to get more vulnerable and tell people about the drugs I had sold and used, the women I had treated poorly, or the thefts committed in my youth. I was worried that sharing those things would make this addiction recovery audience tune me out because I had done things just as bad as, if not worse than, many of them. Since I was also consulting a lot of organizations on marketing and communications, I was also afraid that they would hear these stories and think less of me.

But part of me, deep within, had a feeling that opening up and sharing these stories would benefit audience members that were tuning me out because they thought I was some successful entrepreneur and pastor who had no clue what it was like to have a rough childhood.

So, I took a deep breath and started to share. I told them about the times I'd been afraid, like when we got shot at because my friend changed the prices on the drugs we were selling. I opened up about the shame I felt for the times I'd stolen money from people's houses and cars. I spoke to them about the coldhearted lies I had told women so I could keep them in love with me enough to do whatever I wanted.
And you know what? No one said, "You did what?!" At least not out loud. No one got up and walked away offended. No one came up to me afterwards and called me a hypocrite. In fact, the opposite happened. The energy in the room completely changed. If you've ever been in a room or on stage when everyone was silent and listening to you, then you know exactly the energy I'm referring to.

Suddenly, these people who had been tuning me out were leaning in, nodding. Some, even grown convicted felons, had tears streaming down their faces. They could see themselves in my story, and it gave them hope for what was possible in their lives. The audience, however, weren't the only ones benefiting from my vulnerability.

I was, too.
I was telling the stories that I had a massive amount of shame and embarrassment around, and it was helping others in a powerful way. My relationship to these stories started to shift from embarrassment and shame to empowerment and gratitude. The more I shared, the less shame I felt. The less shame I felt, the more I shared. The more I shared, the more peoples' lives were impacted. The more lives I impacted, the

more confident and grateful I became. The more confident I became, the more I shared the stories—and so on and so forth.

That's the power of expression.

When you give voice and practice to your talents, beliefs, and desires, you release the stored-up energy within that's looking for a place to be expressed.

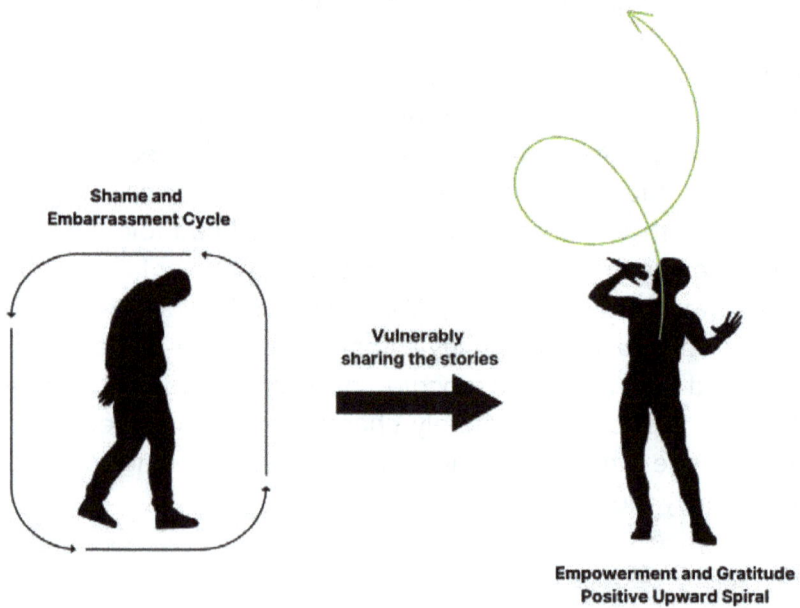

Shame and
Embarrassment Cycle

Vulnerably
sharing the stories

Empowerment and Gratitude
Positive Upward Spiral

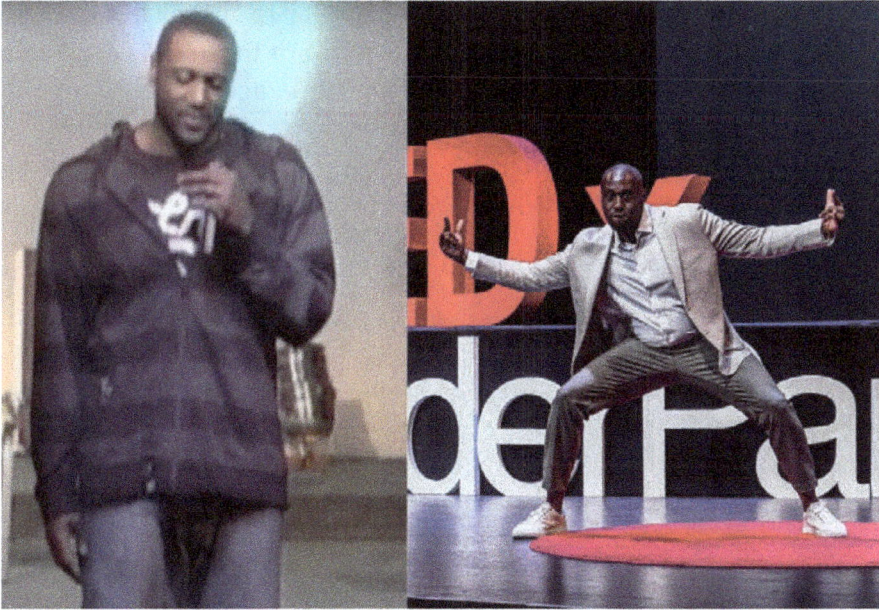

Your skill increases, your belief expands, and your life starts looking more and more like you've dreamed it to be—or beyond.

EXPANDING YOUR EMOTIONAL VOCABULARY

As I was learning to express myself more through public speaking, this Emotion Wheel tool was a game changer. For the longest time, I only had a few words to communicate my emotions: good, sad, angry, pissed, hype, and of course my most popular: "fine" and "not fine." (Side note: Can we please stop saying we are fine if we are not? The way we create a world where it's "okay not to be okay" is by expressing when we are not OK. This makes it safe when others follow suit.)

I would often need to reference an emotional vocabulary resource like The Emotion Wheel to learn how to express emotions I was experiencing.

Without it or a similar resource, it was hard for me or my counselor to get to the root of some of the major challenges I was facing.

This still feels sort of embarrassing to admit, but I've shared this enough from stage to know that I am not alone. There are thousands of people around the world who struggle to know the exact words to use to describe how they feel.

Take a look at an Emotion Wheel. You can also find other versions of these online.

The Junto Institute - Emotion Wheel developed by Robert Plutchik (Plutchik 2001).

The Emotion Wheel can help you identify and articulate your feelings more precisely so you can express them. It's like upgrading from a box of eight crayons to a box of sixty-four—suddenly, you have so many options to choose from.

JOURNALING

Journaling, aka expressing how I feel via writing helped me process my emotions enough to reduce the constant inner turmoil I was in. When I first started journaling, it felt awkward. I didn't know what to write, and I felt so unmanly writing in a diary. But I heard so much about the benefits of journaling that I decided to give it a try.

Some of the benefits I experienced from journaling:
- Emotional clarity

- Reduced stress
- Divine insight
- More effective decision making
- Improved quality of sleep
- Easier ability to forgive
- Deeper gratitude and appreciation
- Increased confidence
- And more...

The benefits I experienced from journaling went far beyond anything I expected. It has become a foundational discipline to my success and fulfillment. My journal helps me gain clarity, anchor gratitude, emotionally release, strategize, create, and focus.

Whenever I talk about journaling like this, someone inevitably rolls their eyes or walks straight up to me and says, "I hear you Darryll, but I'm not really an emotional person."

I always stop them right there and take a moment to explain.

We all have emotions. We all have a voice. Some of us have just gotten really used to suppressing it.

Think back to when you were a baby. The first thing you did when you came into this world was cry. See! You do have emotions! You just have to learn how to access and express them again. Somewhere along your journey, it wasn't safe or acceptable to be emotional, and because of that rejection, we learn to shut that part of ourselves down. We start to think that the conditioned version of ourselves—the one that doesn't show emotion, that always keeps it together—is our true self. But it's not. It's just a mask we've grown comfortable wearing.

A consistent, growing practice of journaling will help you to "thaw emotionally" and step into a new level of expression.

TALK IT OUT

Talking out loud about how I was feeling to express and gain clarity played a major role in my growth of expression. Yes, I was experiencing this growth on stages, but the real work was in my alone time.

I often talk about my problems aloud with God to gain divine perspective and give whatever is within me an outlet. Sometimes I feel God's presence and hear His guidance. Other times, I hear nothing. Regardless of the insight or clarity that may come, I always feel better after verbally expressing and processing.

Counselors can play a major role in holding space for this verbal processing, as well as trusted family and friends. Having a mixture of talking through your feelings out loud by yourself and with others is recommended for maximum benefits.

CREATIVE EXPRESSION

My journey into finding my unique form of expression began with taking personality tests and strength assessments. As I mentioned earlier, I remember taking the StrengthsFinder test and discovering that one of my top strengths was Harmony, the ability to bring people together.

At first, I was frustrated. I was looking around at all these alpha-type leaders and thinking, "How am I supposed to succeed with a strength like that?" But then my instructor gave me an analogy that clicked. He said, "Think of it like playing basketball. If you're a better mid-range shooter than anything else, when you get the ball in that mid-range, take that shot."

That advice led me to join a team-building committee at work. It wasn't glamorous, but it gave me a chance to use my strength. And you know what? People started noticing. They saw how I could connect with different departments and tell stories that brought people together. That opportunity became my gateway to bigger projects, eventually leading to me serving in a major writing and leadership role in one of our largest communication initiatives at the university, affecting millions in revenue.

Your form of expression doesn't have to be what everyone else is doing. It also doesn't have to be something you're passionate about right away either. When I first started public speaking, my passion level was negative ten. I used to jet out of the room during icebreakers and fake like I had to go to the bathroom just so I wouldn't have to talk in front of other people. But as I continued to express myself, I became more confident. My passion for speaking grew, and now my words are impacting people across the globe.

Expressing ourselves has a huge impact on our mental, physical, and emotional health. Research shows that letting our thoughts and feelings out can reduce anxiety and depression. There's a long list of literature that reveals writing about our deepest emotions helps process trauma and lowers stress (Niles et al., 2014). This kind of emotional expression helps us clarify our thoughts and process our emotions, which reduces overwhelm and boosts overall happiness. It's like giving our minds a regular cleanse and uplevel.

Physically expressing ourselves—such as through dance—has also shown to boost our immune system and reduce physical symptoms like headaches and back pain (Tao et al., 2022).

Being open and vulnerable in our emotional expression improves our relationships and communication skills. By sharing our true selves, we create stronger bonds and feel more connected to others.

So, whether through journaling, talking, work, or creative activities, expressing ourselves is a powerful tool for living healthier, happier, more impactful lives.

And here's the beautiful thing: as you start to express yourself, you'll find that you're not just helping yourself. You're giving others permission to express themselves, too. You're creating a ripple effect of authenticity and connection that our world desperately needs.

Try it out:

Here are a few ways you can grow in the practice of giving voice to your talents, beliefs, and desires so that you have increasingly deep fulfillment and give your best to the world.

EXPAND YOUR EMOTIONAL VOCABULARY

- **PAUSE** Take 5-15 minutes at the end of your day to pause and try to pinpoint exactly what you're feeling in the moment.
- **DIG DEEPER** Don't just stop at "happy" or "sad." Are you feeling grateful...? Amazing? Insecure? Frustrated? The more specific you can be, the more you'll gain from this exercise. *Use tools like The Emotion Wheel or Google a list of words to describe emotions to help you if you feel stuck or at a loss for words.
- **SPEAK UP** Now say how you feel out loud. Whatever emotions surge through your body, do your best to allow it vs. fight it.
- **JOURNAL** Briefly journal about what it felt like to express those emotions.
- 7-day streak minimum recommended to see early results.

THE PRACTICE OF JOURNALING

- **SET ASIDE** 10 minutes each day to write.
- **WRITE** about your day, your feelings, your dreams, your fears—whatever comes to mind. Don't worry about grammar, structure, or even if it makes sense. Just let your thoughts flow onto the page. The act of putting your thoughts on paper can be incredibly cathartic and help you process emotions you didn't even know you had.
- **OBSERVE** what comes up. How it made you feel. If you feel better, great! Celebrate! If you feel worse, no worries. Get up, move your body, listen to music that makes you happy, or go do something you enjoy.
- 7-day streak minimum recommended to see early results.

CREATIVE EXPRESSION CHALLENGE!

- **GET IN A SPACE ALONE** where you feel safe, open, and expansive. A large spacious office or nature trail are my favorite two places. I love getting out a large 25x30in flipchart paper to start this challenge.
- **FEELING INTO YOUR HEART**, write down whatever you feel, see, or sense is in your heart. It could be things to do. Places to visit. People to connect with. Silly things. Work things. Whatever comes to mind when you listen to your heart.
- **TAKE ACTION** Spend a minimum of 15 minutes/day doing one or more of the things you wrote on your list, aka expressing yourself. Don't worry about being good at it or making sense of why you're doing what's on your list. The point is to express yourself by doing the things that are in your heart to do — how you see them without judgement from anyone else! This is for you first! Although the world will benefit greatly from your energy.
- **JOURNAL** for 5 minutes at the end of each day about what brought you the most energy and life. Explore why.
- **DO MORE** of the things that make you feel the best.
- 30-day streak minimum recommended to see early results

Remember, do this for yourself first. Express - because whatever is in your heart to be, do, have, or experience is worth saying and pursuing. And if you're like many other caregivers out there, doing it for yourself may not be enough motivation for you to try something as courageous as this Creative Expression Challenge. If so, then think of all the people out there who could benefit from your voice, your gifts, your personality, your light — your essence.

Chapter Six

BREATHE: LET'S BRING IT ALL TOGETHER

Let's face it. Life can be tough. I know what it's like to be seen as successful by everyone around you but feel depressed and miserable when you're alone. I understand the torment of guilt from choices of which you're ashamed. I've experienced the emptiness of drug addiction, where "normal life" feels boring and unfulfilling. I know the feeling of being so disconnected from yourself that your own identity becomes a mystery.

I've felt the pain of betrayal, the weight of defeat, the depths of being lost, and the overwhelming surge of anger and fear that make it unbearable to look at yourself in the mirror. I've known self-hatred so intense that self-inflicted pain felt like punishment I deserved. I, too, have experienced the darkness of wanting to die—of trying to die—and the frustration of surviving, feeling angry at a God I wasn't even sure I believed in.

But... I also know what it's like to survive, to try hard enough, to receive grace, miracles, and support.

I know what it's like to live long enough to see my world completely flipped inside out.

Everyone has a purpose. No matter how big or small. We each play an irreplaceable role in the abundant world we live in.

Today, I've had the joy of speaking to millions of people in person and online. My simple, and yes, dramatic, story has helped people on every continent.

My wife and I just celebrated our 10th year of marriage. We have four of the most awe-inspiring children: Ava, Arianna (Ari), Amaya, and my guy Isaiah. And of course, there's Magic Leo Stinson, our big black-and-white Sheepadoodle in the mix, wagging his giant tail around.

We speak on stages.
We help people share their stories.
We change people's lives.
We stimulate wealth circulation in economies.
We build communities.
We collaborate with others to tackle environmental, domestic abuse, sex trafficking, hunger, poverty, equity, and other pertinent issues.
We travel. We work. We rest. We do *nothing*.
We smile. We cry. We argue. We play.
We run. We walk. We even crawl!
Well, I don't know why we would be crawling. But you get my point!
We're living the "good life." We're blessed and helping others to experience the same.

And by the grace of God, these Self-C.A.R.E. practices have been a major driving force and reason as to why we are able to live this life. In one season, these practices helped me to find enough hope or relief to live another day or sometimes live another minute.

Now they help me prevent self-sabotage, strengthen my relationships, grow my business, expand my paradigm, and stay aligned and true to myself.

This journey you're embarking on isn't about walking around pretending the world is Disneyland, or that you can master sensei your way through anything. It's about actually taking your mental health seriously by developing a system that empowers you to be consistent and intentional with the space you hold — for you.

The System of Self C.A.R.E.

Conscious Awareness · Activities · Relationships · Expression

LET'S RECAP THE CORE OF WHAT WE'VE EXPLORED:

CONSCIOUS AWARENESS:

This is the practice of becoming more consciously aware of how your beliefs influence your behaviors so that you can more effectively and intentionally choose beliefs and behaviors that produce the results you want in life.

Emotional Accounting, Personal Check-Ins, Pattern Tracing, Belief Identification, Mindful Moments and Breathing Exercises are all simple ways to start this practice and strengthen your awareness. Remember, you can't change what you're not aware of. Cultivating this awareness is a powerful step towards your next level of transformation.

ACTIVITIES:

This is the practice of moving your body to get in optimal energetic state so that you have more than enough internal strength, energy and willingness to live and lead at your best. We talked about how movement isn't just about physical health—it's a powerful tool for shifting your mental and emotional state.

Whether it's a two-minute dance party or a mindful walk, start using movement to put yourself in a state that's more conducive to the lifestyle you want to live.

RELATIONSHIPS:

This is the practice of nurturing and deepening your relationship with yourself so that you integrate that beingness into every relationship you have with people, and the world around you.

Remember, the quality of these relationships directly affects your mental health and performance in all areas of life. Nurturing these connections isn't a luxury, it's a necessity. Through exercises like "Me Dates," Mirror

Work, Intentional Relationship Guides, Mindful Eating and the Sixty-Second Challenge, a new level of life will begin to unfold for you.

EXPRESSION:

The practice of giving voice to your talents, beliefs, and desires so that you have increasingly deep fulfillment and give your best to the world.

It's about honoring your authentic self and therefore not living with the mental, emotional, and spiritual weight of being misaligned in one or multiple areas of your life. It's a vital part of maintaining your mental health and living a fulfilled life.

Each of these elements within the practices of Self-C.A.R.E. work together, creating a robust system for thriving personally and professionally. They're tools to help you navigate the complexities of life with more resilience, clarity, and purpose.

<u>As you move forward from here, I want you to remember something crucial</u>: **you matter**. Your experiences, your struggles, your triumphs, your pains, your feelings, your frustrations—they all matter. The world needs the unique gifts that only you can offer. You have within you the power to transform your life, one conscious choice at a time.

Will this journey always be smooth sailing? *Absolutely not.* There will be days when you feel like you're back at square one, days when the old patterns start working their way back into your life. The voice of doubt might whisper: you can't do this, it's too hard, you're not worth the effort. But in those moments, remind yourself that those thoughts are not facts. They're just thoughts, old programs running in the backgrounds of our minds. You have the power to choose what thoughts you think, always.
Enjoy the journey.

Every step, every season—even the detours—matter. No matter how big or small.

Don't underestimate mini moments. Pause for five seconds, breathe, and ask yourself, "How is it that I want to feel right now?"

Self-C.A.R.E. isn't selfish. It's selfless. It's how you bring your best to the world around you.

You don't have to do this work alone. We host a community of authentic, vulnerable, genuine leaders. We teach these practices, storytelling, and much more in our Seeding Greatness Collective Community.

Join the community. This "stuff" is so much easier when you're around others who have similar goals and desires.

No matter what. Keep going.

Stay in the game.

We need you.

You matter.

With everlasting love,
dstints

FREE RESOURCES

Welcome to the Resource section of our self-care workbook, where we've gathered an extensive list of resources designed to support your mental health and performance. In this chapter, you'll find a curated selection of top apps, books, podcasts, Instagram pages, YouTube channels, and websites—all scientifically shown to enhance your self-care journey.

Whether you're looking for guided meditations, insightful books, engaging podcasts, or reliable sources for mental health data, these resources offer a wealth of tools and information to help you manage stress, improve your emotional health, and foster resilience. Jump into these carefully selected options to find additional inspiration and support.

Remember, self-care is a continuous process, and utilizing these resources can help you maintain balance and well-being in your daily life. Explore, experiment, and embrace the practices that resonate with you, knowing that each step you take is a valuable investment in your mental and emotional health.

Download your free resources here!

REFERENCES

Allen, J. G., Romate, J., & Rajkumar, E. (2021). Mindfulness-based positive psychology interventions: a systematic review. *BMC Psychology,* 9(1), 1–116. https://doi.org/10.1186/s40359-021-00618-2

Bor, D. (2013, May 15). Consciousness: Watching your mind in action. New Scientist. https://www.newscientist.com/article/mg21829171-500-consciousness-watching-your-mind-in-action/

Büssing, A., Walach, H., Kohls, N., Zimmermann, F., & Trousselard, M. (2013). Conscious presence and self-control as a measure of situational awareness in soldiers: A validation study. *International Journal of Mental Health Systems,* 7(1), 1–1. https://doi.org/10.1186/1752-4458-7-1

"Carbohydrates and Blood Sugar." (2024). Harvard School of Public Health. https://nutritionsource.hsph.harvard.edu/carbohydrates/carbohydrates-and-blood-sugar/

Holmes, B. (2022). How exercise boosts the brain and improves mental health. Smithsonian Magazine. https://www.smithsonianmag.com/science-nature/how-exercise-boosts-the-brain-and-improves-mental-health-180979511/

Niles, A. N., Haltom, K. E., Mulvenna, C. M., Lieberman, M. D., & Stanton, A. L. (2014). Randomized controlled trial of expressive writing for psychological and physical health: the moderating role of emotional expressivity. Anxiety, stress, and coping, 27(1), 1–17. https://doi.org/10.1080/10615806.2013.802308

Plutchik, R. (2001). The nature of emotions: Human emotions have deep evolutionary roots, a fact that may explain their complexity and provide tools for clinical practice. *American Scientist,* 89(4), 344–350. https://doi.org/10.1511/2001.4.344

Taylor, A. (2021). The Matrix's real-world legacy - from red pill incels to conspiracies and deepfakes. BBC. https://www.bbc.com/news/entertainment-arts-57572152

Tao, D., Gao, Y., Cole, A., Baker, J. S., Gu, Y., Supriya, R., Tong, T. K., Hu, Q., & Awan-Scully, R. (2022). The Physiological and Psychological Benefits of Dance and its Effects on Children and Adolescents: A Systematic Review. Frontiers in physiology, 13, 925958. https://doi.org/10.3389/fphys.2022.925958

Trafton, A. (2019). Two studies reveal benefits of mindfulness for middle school
        students. *MIT News.*
        https://news.mit.edu/2019/mindfulness-mental-health-benefits-students
        -0826

Williamson, M. (1992). *A return to love: Reflections on the principles of a Course
        in miracles* (1st ed.). HarperCollins.

ACKNOWLEDGEMENTS:

THE WORLD'S BIGGEST THANK YOUs!

There are so many people I could thank for getting this material into the world. There are people who deserve credit and applause for how they have influenced me to get to the point where this material could be released.

So, I just want to say thank you to everyone out there who knows you made a difference. And if we've ever crossed paths, you've made a difference. I am so grateful to you.

Now to some specific people...

My Wife, Brittany Stinson

They say the people who are the closest to you are the clearest reflection of yourself. Brittany, you have been with me every day of this self-care journey. I knew you before I even started this process, which is even better because you are a first-hand witness to how this work has changed my life. You have been my reflection, dancing partner, counselor, confidant, writer, parent, strategist, illustrator, editor, encourager—my everything. At this point in my life, there is no me without you. No matter where I go, you are always with me. I love you. Thank you for being you.

My Children

Ava, my first-born—you are me, but so much greater and way more fun! You may have been the clearest reflection, the best opportunity for me to learn how to lead myself. You are full of talent, dreams, and desire. I tell people all the time you need your own team. And yes, me and your mom and your sisters and your brother and our family are all on your team. Thank you for being you. The world will get to benefit from what you made possible.

Arianna, my sweet baby girl! You are a beast. You're just like your mama, but with your own unique flavor. You have been my constant reminder, my example of peace, my opportunity for joy that makes my belly hurt. You are smart, beautiful, and all of the things. I love you, and without you this book would lack structure, clarity, and some common sense. You're the best!

Amaya, my baby girl. From the moment I met you, you changed my life forever. And while I can say that about all your siblings, you specifically demanded an honesty from myself that I really needed — and still do. You are smart, you are gifted, you are kind, you are beautiful, you are feisty, and I love you just as you are. You helped me go deeper in my mirror work. Can you believe that, because of you, people all over the world are going to be way more honest with themselves? Love you and thank you!

Isaiah David Stinson. Geez! It's all in the name. At the time of this writing, you're legit like Jack Jack from the Incredibles—a wild man of many talents. You, my guy, are what they call HIM nowadays! You are HIM! You're the alpha and omega. Without you, there would be a depth and force missing from this work. I love you.

Magic Leo

Our dog. Legit, before him I was too much in my head during my walk and talks. It's something about his effect that helped me stay in more of a flow, processing, and listening, receiving, and I don't know, it's magic. He does often come on tour with us, and for the lucky ones who get to meet him, he has this effect on them, too. Still, he deserves it: thank you and love you, Magic Leo.

My Parents and Family

Mom, Dad, Grandma Greta, Bre, Bernie, Van, Nacole, Ashlee, Chas, David, Grandma D., Stacey, DeShawn, Auntie Dwyla, Jimmy, Jodi, Rick—please don't make me name all y'all. Y'all are my roots and my inspiration. There is no me without you. Love you, forever!

And yes mom. You, and my grandmother are in a category all by y'all selves! Your love, prayers, faith, and sacrifice will forever be my foundation.

Pops, you are too. Our talks. Your mentorship, friendship, and loving sacrifice changed my entire world for the better. I'm so grateful to have you as my father.

Alexis Snell

You were an angel divinely sent to support this project. Without you, thousands... if not millions of people would never receive this material because of how less I would have promoted it knowing the interior didn't more accurately reflect my heart. I'm honestly in tears writing this right now in deep gratitude for how you showed up and served despite having a busy work load and plenty reasons to say "now isn't the best time." Thank you! You're a real one.

Amber Vilhauer

Name 1 person who will lend you one of their top staff members in the middle of running two major events where all hands on deck are required. You trusted me. You trusted Alexis. You showed up and gave, like you always do, and the world will never be the same because of it. You are #infiniteimpact.

Kristen McCall

Part of getting creative work out into the world requires the freedom to fully express and explore. You enabled me to do that with your amazing artistic gifts, and willingness to go back and forth, and back and forth and back and forth. Without you, I would have been stuck in a pity party and never tapped into my full expression that made this book possible. Thank you.

To Amanda Catarzi, my first editor of this book.

You were the spark and support this book needed to get started. There's still a bit of you sprinkled in! Before we connected, I was so overwhelmed with all the ideas in my head about this book. You helped me process and helllllldd sooooomee spppaaacccccceee my girl! You helped me put pen to paper and jumpstart the process to get this material to the world. Thank you for your time, energy, effort, skill, and heart. Much luv!

Dorothy Francis, a.k.a. Grandma D,

Wow! You absolutely nailed the fine edits of this book. It's like the

Christmas tree was decorated. It was big and amazing in itself. You came with the ornaments, the garland, and all the finishing touches to make it look perfect, and added shining bright lights and a beautiful North Star on the top! That's what you did to elevate this material! I owe you the world, and I will be eternally grateful for your service. Thank you so much; love you forever.

To my coaches, mentors, pastors, and friends
Thank you for who you know you are to me. You each know what that means for you specifically. I love you beyond what I have words to express.

To you, reading this
Welcome to the fam! If you've read this far, you're with us for life! I can't wait to connect.

I'm looking forward to whatever lies before us!

Let's get it!

ABOUT THE AUTHOR

Darryll Stinson is the co-founder of Seeding Greatness, a movement of leaders restoring the planet and helping humanity to heal through their stories and transformational services.

As a former Division 1 athlete, Darryll overcame multiple suicide attempts to become a best-selling author and 2xTEDx speaker with more than two million views. His accolades as a Top 100 athlete (2008), award-winning higher ed communications professional, #9 Suicide Awareness Speaker (2023), and TEDx organizer (2022-present), attest to the impact of his work.

He's coached hundreds of speakers to reach millions of people while growing themselves and their business at the same time.

When he's not coaching or captivating audiences, Darryll enjoys rapping, reading, and spending quality time with his wife, Brittany, his children, Ava, Arianna, Amaya, Isaiah, and his dog, Magic.

www.ingramcontent.com/pod-product-compliance
Lightning Source LLC
Chambersburg PA
CBHW071234090426

42736CB00014B/3077